# 101 Ways to Piss Off Your Cashier

## By Kayla McCaskey

# DEDICATION

Dedicated to all the cashiers at Mount Washington Shop n Save. Thank you for your help listing pet peeves and I hope you enjoy the book.

# Introduction

After 6 years of working a cash register, I have noticed a lot of ways that customers just don't care. We get that everyone has their days. The main problem is how people act while doing the things that push our buttons. The problem isn't the peeves themselves, necessarily. The truth is, if you have a good attitude we really don't care what you do. Showing up at the register and giving a bad immediate impression is what causes us cashiers to seem like we hate you. It is a minimum wage job, normally. If you know anything about minimum wage, you will understand that we don't want to be there to begin with. Honestly, the money is hardly worth the time and effort we expend on it. When we come to work knowing we will make maybe $50 and have to deal with all sorts of problems from customers, it really sucks. To help our customers see things from our point of view, I decided to write this book. I divided it into five chapters: What you do personally, anything to do with money, how you treat your cashier, bagging issues, and random things that are just plain annoying. I hope it helps people understand it's not easy being at the bottom of the totem pole.

# Part 1
# Personal

1. Phones/earbuds

   This one is a preferential problem among cashiers. While we find it annoying that you ignore us to gossip or listen to a song that you could easily pause, when you show you don't care enough to pay attention, we take it as a break from small talk.

   Example: Who am I kidding? Everybody does it!

   Moral of this story: hang up the phone and pay for your groceries!

2. Vanishing but leaving groceries on the belt

   When you are only buying like 4 items but you realize you forgot to grab a fifth, take your groceries with you. Technically, you are not finished shopping. By leaving your purchases on the belt, you not only chance holding up the line, but you are essentially wasting everyone's time while they are stuck waiting for you. We get that you don't want to wait in line again, but that is why coming prepared with a shopping list comes in handy. Also, do not leave your husband to guard your merchandise. We then have that awkward five minutes where we either have to entertain him or stare off into space while he smiles at us.

   Example: A guy left two boxes of pasta and some peanut butter on the belt. He disappeared to go to the other side of the store and get a frozen pizza. I had to ring up his groceries awhile. Angry customers kept leaving my line and going to another register because they don't have time to wait for him to walk all the way back to the register.

Moral: take your groceries with you if you forgot something, or at least do not put them on the belt.

3. Nagging about price checks

This is one of my personal biggest pet peeves. We understand that you want to save money in this economy, we all want to. However, when the item rings up the wrong price and you inform us, we immediately get to work solving the problem. When you keep talking about it, shoving the store advertisement in my face, all I want is for you to shut up. We promise we will take care of the problem, but you have to let us actually get a chance to do so.

Example:

Customer: "Miss, this meat is supposed to be buy one get one free,"

Me: "Okay, let me call the meat department and double check,"

Customer: "Miss, it is right here in the store advertisement. Here, look," proceeds to shake the store ad in my face until I take it and look at it.

Me: "I understand that, but we still have to make sure you got the meat that is on sale and that it is fixed in the system if it is the right one."

Customer continues to nag me while I try to take care of their order.

Moral: Let me do my job and please don't nag me while I'm doing it.

4.  Having an attitude

    This one is just common sense. We are stuck at our minimum wage job taking crap from customers. When you come in line acting like we ruined your day, you are ruining ours. Once again, we understand people have their days when they just don't want to deal with people. If you don't like the cashier, go in another line. If you have heard rumors about a cashier, try not to judge them since you really don't know the truth. Otherwise, just try to remember we don't want to be there anymore than you want to chat with us. However, we have a job to do, so please let us do it.

    I don't think I need an example of this one.

    Moral: if you give me an attitude, things can only go downhill from there.

5.  Telling us exactly how much every item costs

In most grocery stores, the price is already in the system. When you tell us that something is 2 for $3, we really do not need to know that. To be honest, we completely forget what you said the price was as soon as you tell us. Unless the price comes up as something ridiculously overpriced, we don't need to pay attention to the specific sales. Do yourself a favor and just watch the monitor. If it doesn't ring up correctly, just tell us one time (as previously talked about) and we will take care of it.

Example:

Customer: "This is buy one get one free, that is 5 for $10, this is $3.99".

Moral: Don't worry about telling us prices, the system takes care of that for us.

6. Mumbling or not speaking English

I constantly have to tell certain customers that I cannot understand them. If you are too quiet, mumbling, or not speaking English that makes our job a whole lot more difficult. Communication is an important part of the cashier-customer relationship. If we don't talk to you, you report us for being rude. If we can't understand you, you may as well not talk at all. If we have to ask you to speak up or speak more clearly so many times, we might just stop caring and ignore everything you are saying.

Example: if I had one, this wouldn't be a problem.

Moral: Speak up, speak clearly, speak English

7. Whistling/humming/making animal noises

When you get in line and you are whistling, it makes it very difficult for us to communicate with you.

For some reason, people love to shop while mooing or making bird sounds. It is just plain obnoxious and you sound very immature.

Example: A guy comes to the register humming. I have a headache and I can't communicate with him because he is too busy humming to respond.

Moral: Make noise at home, not in public

8. Leaving your keys at the register

We do not enjoy racing outside trying to catch you, whether you left your keys or some groceries. It saves us all some time and energy if you make sure you do not leave your belongings sitting around. Plus, you are not going to get very far without your keys so save yourself another trip into the building.

Example: I don't think you need an example of this one. It is pretty self-explanatory.

Moral: Keep your groceries close, and your keys closer.

9.  Public Displays of Affection

    We understand you are in love and can't keep your hands off each other. However, it really only takes five minutes to ring you up so please get through it without touching. Some of us are stuck working when we would like nothing more than to be at home with our significant others. Others of us don't have anyone to go home to and having to watch you be all lovey dovey is just heart breaking. It is also really gross to watch people suck face instead of sliding their payment card.

    Example: I don't want to read about it either, so let's not.

    Moral: Hands off until you get home.

10. Body Odor

    This one seems like a no-brainer but sadly, we still have to spray air fresheners after some people leave the store. If we look like we can't breathe, we probably can't. Shower, use deodorant, and if you want to wear perfume or cologne, use one spray. Seriously, I know people who can work out every day, don't shower for three days, and still don't stink. I really do not know how these people are managing to smell bad.

Example: Catman, as we call him. He always come into the store wearing the same sweatshirt. He always has ear buds in and buys about ten groceries. We always fight about who has to ring him up. We always discreetly turn away so we can catch our breath while ringing him up. We always have to spray air freshener after he leaves.

Moral: Take a shower or spray yourself with air freshener.

11. Giving out your personal information

A lot of my coworkers complain about this one. A customer will tell them their address or try to give them their phone number.

We are just there to do our job and go home. We are not interested in meeting up with you after work or calling you especially since most of you are twice our age. There's a word for that: creepy.

Example: I think we get it.

Moral: Don't trust us with that information, we really don't want to know.

12. Leaving your receipt at the register

There are trash cans at the exit. Even if you don't feel like throwing it away yourself, you could at least let us know and hand the receipt to us to throw away for you. Ditching the paper at the bottom of the register is much the same as littering. It makes the store look trashy and gives us more work to do.

13. Small talk

We understand that it is our job to provide good customer service. That does not mean we need to talk about the weather a thousand times a shift. Also, if we are there we are obviously having an okay day. When you ask how we are, we both know everyone is going to say good and then probably have an awkward silence. Why waste our breath? Just say hi, thank you, and have a nice day. This is very important when we are in the middle of a rush and have six people waiting in line. We just want to get you taken care of and get you on your way home as quickly as possible. That's not rude, that's being efficient.

Example:

Customer: "I have to go here and get this and then go there and do that, I'm so thirsty so I came here first for a carton of tea."

Me: Just smile and nod, smile and nod

Moral: Keep it moving, we've got work to do.

14. Expecting us to tell you the total

We know some of you cannot see well enough to read the total yourselves. However, if you can't read the total you probably are not reading this book. As for the rest of you, the total is right there. Standing there waiting for us to actually say it out loud when we already know you read it yourself, makes you look rude and bossy. For the most part, we do tell our customers the total. Every so often we need a moment of silence. Whether it is because we haven't had a drink in a while during the rush or we are just tired, there's a reason we haven't told that one-in-twenty customer the total. We appreciate if you can let us have that little break.

Example:

Customer: "Ahem, ahem. What's my total?" She nudges her head toward the screen where the total is clearly printed.

Moral: Don't be obnoxious about it. If we know you can see it, we aren't going to say it.

15. Being mean when your team loses

Seriously, we are all sad that the team lost. It happens, though. Remember we didn't even get to see the game so it really is not fair to take out your frustration on us. Save the anger for in front of your television screen.

16. Screeching/ whining children

We know there are exceptions and we can't always expect peace and quiet when there are children in the store. That doesn't make it any less annoying. I bet all the moms reading this are rolling their eyes saying yeah, like we enjoy our kids being obnoxious. I'm just agreeing with you. And, hey, this is all about the ways our customers drive us crazy. That's one of the ways so I am including it.

Example:

Child: "I want this! I want that!"

Parent: "No, I can't afford it."

Moral: Explain how much things cost and how much people make. I bet if kids understood money they would stop whining for you to spend it. I know I would have.

# Part 2
# Money

1. Buying more than you can afford

It takes a lot of time and effort to fix something that could have been taken care of simply by paying attention to the shelf prices as you picked up each grocery. Even if you just tell your cashier how much you have, at least we know to stop at a certain price then.

Example: There was this one couple who always got two full carts of groceries when they only had $200. I got news for you! That money only goes so far in this economy! They had every single item rung up before they bothered to tell us they only had so much money. We had to restart the whole transaction and they had to pick and choose out of 400 groceries which 150 they wanted the most.

Moral: Bring a calculator or count in your head as you go.

2. Anything involving WIC

WIC may be the most annoying transaction a cashier will ever encounter. First, we have to make sure you bought the right brands. Then, we have to look at the size. Even if you pick up everything correctly, it may not be WIC allowable in our system, so then we have to wait for a manager to put it in the computer so we can finally finish your transaction. By the way, NO we cannot substitute different eggs because you think we are out of the WIC ones. I promise we are never out of the WIC eggs. We get such an attitude from our WIC customers, it is unbelievable.

Example: One of the worst customers I ever had asked me to substitute Eggland's Best for Hillendale Grade A Large (the WIC eggs). When I told her "Ma'am, I have worked with WIC for 6 years and I know that is not how WIC works, there are no substitutions," she then snapped back at me, "This is when you go up to the courtesy desk and ask your boss if I can substitute these eggs!" I was appalled and told her they were only going to say the same thing I already said but she insisted. I asked my boss and she said exactly the same thing I said. Then, she went and got the customer the correct eggs that she had claimed we were out of.

Moral of this story: We do know how to do our jobs. Please respect that.

3. Swiping payment card wrong

This one seems like rocket science to a lot of people. It really is pretty simple. The black strip on the card always needs to be in the machine. The part that sticks up with numbers on it does not. Every time someone tries to swipe the indented part of their card, they make the machine a little less usable.

4. Asking for specific bills with cash back

If you are taking the bus or subway, you probably will need change. The problem with that is everybody and their mother is asking for the maximum cash back amount. We do not have an infinite supply of money, although we would love to think we do.

Example:

Customer asks for a 5, four 1 dollar bills, and four quarters. The next customer asks for three 5 dollar bills and five 1 dollar bills. The next customer pays with a hundred dollar bill for a $15 purchase.

Moral: Put your money on a Connect card so you don't need change. If you are doing laundry, go to courtesy and ask for a roll of quarters.

5.   Expired coupons

Many times we find that a customer has a pile of about fifty coupons and twenty of those coupons are expired. We are not sure if you do it on purpose or are just not checking before you come shopping. We do get in trouble for taking bad coupons so if you are trying to be sneaky you will get caught.

Moral: Check your coupons ahead of time. Also, honesty is the best policy.

6.   Complaining you are poor on welfare

When a customer comes up to the register with a cart full of groceries, we think there are two possibilities. Either you get a lot of help from SNAP, you lucky person you, or you actually made that much money and are paying with credit or debit. Those of you who fall under the second part, we applaud you. Those of you who have SNAP have one huge problem in common: you still whine that you are broke. Maybe I'm a little biased because I have made several attempts to get on welfare and never succeeded which is very upsetting and frustrating. Those of us working at cash registers, and you can bet me any money this is true, do not make enough to eat steak even once a week. We are just glad to pay rent and a phone bill if we have a phone. We live on fifty cent bags of chips and seventy-five cent cartons of tea while on the clock. The point is: we really do not need to hear you whining when at least you can feed yourself.

Example:

Customer: "I can't get seafood AND filet mignon?"

Cashier: "You can if you put back some of your snack foods."

Customer: "I'll just get some cake."

Moral: Be mindful because you are actually doing better than the rest of us.

7.  Forgetting your perks card

One of your biggest complaints is that we do not accept phone numbers when you forget your perks cards. The most annoying part of that is when you come up to us and just start listing your phone number. We then have to stop you so we can fill you in on our store policies. The sales at the store are the actual prices for the most part so you do not actually need your card to get sale prices (which is what freaks out most people that forgot their card). If you want fuel perks, you should just bring your card back with your receipt that totaled at least five dollars excluding tobacco or milk purchases. Otherwise, you will still get the sales.

Moral: Remember your card.

8.  You can't find your money

You come to the register only to realize you suddenly have no idea where you put your money. While you stand there, rummaging through all your pockets and bags, a line is starting up. The best part is when you leave your money in the car.

Example:

Customer: "I left my money in the car. I will be right back."

Cashier has to decide if they are going to suspend the transaction or wait for the customer to come back into the store. Meanwhile, cashier has to keep explaining to other customers why they will probably want to go to another register.

Customer comes back: "It was in my pocket the whole time."

Moral: Come prepared.

9.   Not knowing your welfare card balance

When you come to the register with a SNAP card and you don't know how much is on it, it takes a lot longer for us to get you on your way home. First, we have to ring up all your groceries, then you swipe the card, last if it declines we now know how much you have but we have to take off some groceries and restart the whole payment process. If your card does not swipe, we are stuck typing in your card number over and over. It is not easy since there is no backspace button. One mistake and we have to start all over. After all that, there is a line behind you.

Moral: Come prepared.

10.  Giving extra change after we open the till

Most people do not enjoy math a whole lot. We would rather let the register tell us exactly how much money we owe you. When we type in your amount and the till opens so we can get you change, you handing us more change just makes it all the harder.

Example: Total is $5.83 and customer gives cashier $5.90. Cashier opens till to get the customer's change, but the customer hands them three pennies so they can get a dime back.

Moral: Decide your change before the till opens.

11. Disorganized multiple payments

When you come in line with a bunch of groceries and can only afford it by paying with four different payments, we absolutely need to know ahead of time. The computers make us use certain payments in certain orders so if we are misinformed we have to get a manager to finish the transaction.

Example: Customer has to pay with a gift card, a credit card, SNAP cash, and SNAP food. Cashier needs to use SNAP food first and SNAP cash last.

Moral: Make sure you communicate multiple methods of payment.

12.  Money is everywhere/ all bent up

When you come in line and you are unorganized, you are probably one of those people who end up dropping a big pile of bent up bills on the counter. We then have to take the time to pick up, straighten, and count all the bills. Depending on how much your bill is, that could take a while and leave us with a long line.

Moral: Get organized.

13. Putting cash on the counter when our
    hand is out

When we see you paying cash, we always put our hand out to take them. There is a reason we do that. We are not being rude; we simply have a very hard time getting bills and coins up off the smooth counter top. Half of us do not have nails, which leaves us struggling to get anything flat off the counter.

Moral: Hand us your money, don't lay it anywhere.

14. Money is sweaty/gross

The most disgusting thing we have to do is take money from you when you just took it out of your bra on a humid summer day. Another disgusting thing is when you lick your finger to separate each bill. First, we have a sponge you are welcome to use to wet your fingers. Second, those bills are covered in germs so you are probably inviting some nasty virus into your body when you lick your finger, touch a bill, lick your finger again, and so forth.

Moral: Keep your money dry.

15. SNAP card that doesn't swipe

This one we can't blame on you (unless you are one of those people who sat on your card and snapped it in half) but it is still annoying and time consuming so we are including it. When your SNAP card won't swipe, we have to type all those digits into the computer ourselves. Without a backspace button, that can be pretty aggravating. It can take five tries to finally type in the entire number correctly. If you accidentally mess up the transaction on your end and we have to type it in again, that's even worse. It is annoying and usually ends with us having a little line.

Moral: Apply for a new card.

16. Paying a $100 bill for less than $10 worth of groceries

It sucks when you come to a register with all hundred dollar bills. Especially if we just did a pick-up, then we probably have only one $20 bill in our till. We then have to give you a bunch of tens and probably fives as well. As soon as you leave, we have to get a loan for all the money we just gave away.

Moral: Use smaller bills.

## 17. Paying in all change

Saving up a crap load of change for emergencies is only a good idea if you put it into rolls or go to a Coin Star. The problem with change is that you usually dump it on our register from a baggie and then you try to count for us when we have to count it anyway. It ends up taking twice as long as you would expect. It also gives us more work to do when it is the end of the night and you choose to pay this way. Remember, we have to count all that money over and over. It is not fun.

Moral: Go to a Coin Star or don't pay all in change.

## 18. Claiming we gave you the wrong change back

When we give you your change, do us a favor and count it. If you think we messed up, check your receipt to make sure you know how much change you were supposed to get. If there is still a problem, recount your change. Nine times out of ten we are not the ones making mistakes. We know how valuable every cent is and when you claim we are messing up, we feel like you are picking on us or saying we can't count.

Moral: Count your change very carefully.

## 19. Throwing money at us

This is obviously only for customers who are impatient or in a bad mood. Otherwise, why would you be throwing anything at anyone, right? We get that you are upset, but please don't throw money at us. First of all, if the cash touches up the right way, we could get a paper cut. Plus, money is full of germs so the cut would probably get infected.

Moral: Do not throw money at your cashier.

20. Ignoring questions we ask you

When you are at the register and the cashier asks you if you are using credit or debit, there is a reason for that. We know you already answered all the questions on the machine. We cannot put your payment through unless you prove who you are. If you are entering a pin, we obviously do not need any more proof than that. It is when you pay with credit and expect to walk out after simply swiping any random card that we need proof. It is so easy to steal an identity these days. You would think people have gotten smarter and we have nothing to check, but we do get complaints of credit card fraud. That is why we have to see identification. Ignoring it will not make us give you the easy way out. If you do not want to show identification, pay with debit or go somewhere else. Definitely do not give us attitude, though.

Moral: Don't ignore any questions when you can't leave until you answer them.

21. Handing us your card

There is a machine for you to swipe your payment card through. We cannot do anything for you, so do not try to hand us your payment card. There are some customers who demand we finish the transaction for them because they do not know how to use their own payment card. If you don't know how to use it, why do you even have it? There are times when you are in your own world and hand us your card out of habit. That is fine since we will let you know to swipe your card yourself.

Moral: Learn how to use credit and debit.

# Part 3

## Cashier Etiquette

1. Getting in personal space

This is one of the most annoying things you do to us. When we are standing in our area and there is suddenly a butt pressed against ours, we do not appreciate that. This happens more than you may think. Not only is it scary to be touched by a stranger when we least expect it, but we try very hard not to be rude. That means we are stuck standing very still while we wait for you to pull your butt in.

Example: An older lady with back problems puts her groceries too far into her cart. When she reaches the register, she finds she cannot reach half of her things. With her butt sticking a foot out behind her, touching the cashier trying to work at the next register, she empties her cart.

Moral: Be more aware of the people around you.

2. Handing us groceries

You may think you are helping us when you hand us groceries, but it actually makes our jobs harder. We know exactly where that item was on the belt, but suddenly it is not there anywhere. We then play a mini game of tag trying to get the grocery from you so we can scan it.

Moral: Once the food is out of your cart, leave it alone until we hand it to you bagged.

3. Not unloading your own basket

This is one of our biggest pet peeves of all. It is common sense that when you use a cart you empty that yourself. It goes the same way with baskets. You fill it, you empty it. We have all sorts of excuses to get you to empty your basket nicely. My favorite is that I have carpal tunnel and it hurts my wrists to empty baskets all day. The truth is, it is not easy reaching up and over the brim of the basket to get your groceries out for you.

Example: One of the funniest incidents ever:

Customer sets his basket on my register. He proceeds to stand there staring into space. As I am finishing my current customer, I ask him to empty his basket awhile. He slams each item down onto the belt. When the basket is empty, he throws it on the ground stating that he is not going to put it away.

Moral: No one is asking you to put your baskets away. If you choose to do so, thank you, but that is your own choice. We are simply asking a little help from our customers. So, please empty your baskets.

4.  Telling us how to bag

This really gets under my skin. We already know to wrap protective plastic around your chicken. We do not need you to tell us how to do that. Nor do we need to be reminded to put cleaning supplies in a separate bag. We understand that if we bag it wrong and it leaks, we will have poisoned and possibly killed a customer. Now, if you want very specific bagging, please just do it yourself. It saves us both the headache and the possible hard feelings.

Moral: Tell us from the start or let us do it the way we were taught.

5.  Bossing us around

This goes hand in hand with the bagging problem. If you are picky and want your groceries bagged a certain way, your best bet is to do the bagging yourself. Those of us who are young are really tired of being bossed around and the elder cashiers obviously know how to carry their own weight.

Moral: Bag your own nit-picks.

6.  Acting like my best friend

There is a big difference between being friendly and being too friendly. Don't come to the register and ask all sorts of questions about our lives. Especially if we do not know you, it makes us think we need to keep an eye on you in public.

Example:

Customer: "Did you have a nice weekend?"

Cashier: "Well, I was working, so I don't think so."

Customer: "You hate your job, then?"

Moral: Do not play 20 questions with your cashier.

7.  Not returning your unwanted items to their shelves

At the end of the day we find liters of soda stuffed into the candy racks, bags of chips on top of coolers, boxes of pasta hidden in baskets under the register, and lots of other things. The problem is, we have to find all the items you hide and put them away. Days later, we find a half a cantaloupe growing mold. Things like that are not necessary. If you don't want something, put it back where you found it. It takes thirty seconds to cross the entire room so you can't possibly be in too much of a hurry. Plus, you should not have picked it up if you were not sure in the first place.

Moral: If you absolutely have to bring unwanted groceries to the register, hand them to us, don't hide them on the candy racks.

8. Staring at us

Huge creep alert and this happens constantly. Usually it is one of you older gentlemen and we are sorry to say but you staring only makes us want to throw up. You might think we are pretty but you need to respect that and look away. Also, your fellow customers do tell us when you sneak a peek at our butts. Either way, it is disrespectful.

Moral: Take a picture, it will last longer.

9. Choosing to come in our line just because we are eating

If we are eating it is simply because we cannot wait any longer to eat. When you interrupt our emergency snack, we get very upset. It is not easy staying well-nourished when we only get one fifteen minute break a day. Please, do not interrupt just because you want to make a stupid comment. Yes, we are eating. Why do you care what it is we are eating? Yes, we are allowed to eat on the job!

Moral: We are human so let us eat.

### 10. Ignoring us for the Redbox

We know you want a movie to take home. When you are at the register closest to the Redbox and we are trying to get your transaction finished, don't walk to the Redbox and ignore us. You may think you have a minute to look at it while we ring you up, but we are faster than you would expect.

Moral: Pay first, then pick a movie.

### 11. Ignoring us for your friends

You see someone you haven't seen in a while and you get excited, we get that. You want to catch up on ten years of life in five minutes? That is not going to happen without you ignoring us. That means we are probably standing there for about five minutes trying to get your attention and the person you are talking to has to eventually let you know we are waiting.

Moral: Pay first, and then chat with your friends.

### 12. Racism/False accusations of racism

Sometimes you can really upset us and we ignore you or are slightly rude back to you. This does not make us racist, it makes us human. If you come in my line and I don't talk, don't automatically think it has something to do with the color of your skin. This is Pittsburgh, for crying out loud. If you are racist in Pittsburgh, you will never survive. When we ask you if you are paying with food stamps, it is not because of your skin color. We had to learn a less offensive way to ask you simple questions so we would not be accused of racism. If we do something that offends you enough to think we are racism, ask us what you did and we responded the way we did. I promise it is never about your skin color.

Moral: You will be treated as you treat us, it doesn't matter what color you are.

13. Asking my name

Some of us have stopped wearing our name tags at work because that is a privacy issue in this day and age. Some one knows your first name and where you work, they can find out everything else. Soon you either have a stalker on your hands or your identity has been stolen. This is why we do not tell you our names. We really do not understand why you need to know our names to begin with. Asking for a name means one of two things: 1-you like us and are going to say something creepy or religious and 2- you want to report us for something silly that we don't do intentionally to upset you. Either way, it is not necessary.

Moral: Be nice but not personal.

14. "Tipping" with change

When we hand you your change, you should thank us and leave with your groceries. There is no reason to hand us the pennies back and call it our tip. It is rude and seems disrespectful. We have enough trouble getting by on minimum wage; we don't need a customer sarcastically offering us more money.

Moral: If you don't want your pennies, just say so. Don't make rude jokes.

## 15. Snatching

Whether it is money or bags of groceries, this is extremely rude. You are probably upset at us for one reason or another but just remember we have to put up with a lot and at some point we stop caring if it upsets someone. Snatching money can cause paper cuts and hurt feelings. Either way, it is not a great idea. Also, some cashiers have their own way of doing their job. If we decide to ring your grocery and immediately bag it, we are being efficient. We find it very annoying when we are trying to finish loading a bag and you are trying to take it from us. If you don't want anything else in that bag, say something. Otherwise, wait until we have let go of the handles to take the bag. It really is not making things go faster and you are not being helpful.

Moral: Take your time and don't be rude.

## 16. Acting superior

If this book were written in ranking order, this would be number one. It is absolutely the worst feeling in the world to be treated badly because we work minimum wage. The fact is, someone has to do it and if you already have the good jobs then you should thank your lucky stars. We haven't settled, failed out of high school, or done anything stupid to get here. We are trying to survive just like everyone else. Most of us are constantly looking for second jobs or a better job because we know working at a grocery store is not a great job. Think about that next time you degrade us when we make a mistake.

Moral: No one is too good to work in a grocery store. It could have been you.

17. Commentary on anything we do

This comes off as obnoxious to us when we are trying to fake a smile and get through our day. When you come to us and point out food on our faces or the fact that we are eating, these are terrible conversation starters. We probably already know because our coworkers tell us without sounding extremely rude. You sound like the obnoxious neighbor everyone avoids.

Moral: Leave out the rude comments.

18. Threats

Thankfully, this does not happen often. However, when we are joking around with you and you out of nowhere threaten to never shop here again or tell our manager we are rude, that takes the fun out of our jobs. Plus, we were raised to take threats very seriously. Telling us you will shoot us if we don't give you a discount is scary and we can't give you one anyway. There are cops coming in and out of the store constantly, so it won't be funny when they hear a cashier being threatened.

Moral: Don't threaten people, it is illegal.

19. Ignorant comments

This one goes hand in hand with the commentary part. Some days we aren't our best and we apologize. However, there is no need to point out our imperfections. If we drink something and it makes our teeth red, don't point it out. If we have a little facial hair or got a spot on our shirt, we still have to get through the shift. You make it almost impossible for us to keep working when you embarrass us with comments.

Moral: Notice but don't talk about things.

20. Asking the manager after we have already answered

This is pretty much treating us like we are inferior. When you come to a register, expect us to know what we are doing. If we don't, we are not afraid to ask our supervisors for assistance. If you ask us a question and you don't like the answer, do not turn around and ask the manager right in front of us. You are wasting everyone's time as well as being rude.

Moral: Ask your cashier anything and expect they will help you.

21. Asking if we are open

If you are looking to pay for your groceries and you see a register with no line, the number lit up, and a cashier standing behind it, put your groceries on the belt. You look stupid and waste time asking. If the light is on, the line is open. If someone left the light on and walked away, they are probably bagging while they wait for their own customers. We get a lot of people claiming there was no one to ring them up and all you did was walk by. If you put your groceries on the belt of a register that has no sign of being closed, we will take care of you. Asking us if we are open when we are standing there waiting for a customer makes us want to respond rudely. One of these days, I am going to tell a customer I'm just standing there for my health.

Moral: If we look open we are open.

# Part 4
# Bagging

1. Requesting blue bags

Pittsburgh has this weird rule that you cannot recycle unless it is in a blue bag. We sell blue bags in the garbage bag aisle. Some of you are trying to save money and we get that. However, when we have a loaded bag rack or have already begun bagging your groceries, asking for blue bags is very annoying. We really don't have a lot of them because they are probably more expensive for the store to provide and you take as many as you can every time. Another problem is that blue bags are more slippery for some reason, so it makes a mess when we have to take blue bags out from under white bags.

Moral: Buy your own recycling bags.

2. Requesting paper and plastic

We understand that the elderly have trouble carrying heavy loads and need extra support from paper bags. However, some of you like to get paper and plastic for a bushel of bananas. It takes forever to get the paper to open correctly inside the plastic bags. With how the economy seems to work these days, the more-environmentally-safe paper bags are probably more expensive than the harmful plastic bags. Save the Earth and save the store some money so they might be able to lower food prices. Also, reaching up, over, and down into those bags is quite a workout. Some of us workout on a daily basis and we still feel the burn from holding our arms up so high to fill your paper bags. We know a little exercise never hurt anyone.

Moral: Help us bag or just get plastic.

   3.   Rebagging what we already bagged

We take serious offense when you go through the bags and take them apart. We have to take the time to bag your groceries and we are pretty good at doing so. If you want things bagged a particular way, either let us know or bag it yourself. You look rude and waste a lot of precious time undoing work we already did.

Moral: Leave our bagging alone!

   4.   Requesting bagging after we have already bagged

When we have just handed you your receipt or have finally finished bagging your six bags worth of groceries, we expect to be finished with that part of the transaction. If you suddenly decide you want paper and plastic, you make our job take way longer. Not only does it hold up the line, it makes us strain ourselves again.

Moral: Decide your bagging methods ahead of time.

   5.   Grabbing bags from other registers

Most of us take a lot of time to organize our bags. Then you come through and pull the bags off without looking to see if you made a mess. You almost always make a mess when you do that. Our bags do not like to stay attached to the rest of the bags, so we end up with accordion-style bags hanging from the stand. The best part is when you grab the bag we were just reaching for. That is simply rude and we might have to get more bags.

Moral: Have your cashier provide your bags.

6. Paper and plastic for one item

We laugh at each other when we see a coworker ring up a customer who wants their newspaper in paper and plastic. Paper bags are there to make carrying a heavy load sturdy. You probably do that so you can use the paper for other things, but it just looks obnoxious and takes us forever.

Moral: Save paper, take plastic for one item.

7. Not helping bag a huge cart load

When you empty your cart from an overflowing mountain to the bottom, we run out of space on the register. When that happens, we not only could use some help, we need you to put your rung up bags into your cart. It is a lot of work to scan and bag a ton of groceries as quickly as we can, so we would appreciate if you help us with the bagging. Plus, you usually end up with a lot more bags if you let us bag it all ourselves. We don't know if you want the bags loaded or easy to carry so we make them easy to carry.

Moral: Help your cashier out a little.

www.ingramcontent.com/pod-product-compliance
Lightning Source LLC
Chambersburg PA
CBHW071008180526
45168CB00003B/1338